The Most Unusual Pet Ever:

Henry, Our Great Blue Heron

and His Adventures

The Most Unusual Pet Ever: Henry, Our Great Blue Heron and His Adventures

WRITTEN BY **Sondra Perry**

ILLUSTRATED BY **Janice Byer**

Second Edition

JABBERWOCKY MINNEAPOLIS

Jabberwocky Press
212 3rd Avenue North, Suite 290
Minneapolis, MN 55401
612.455.2293
www.Jabberwocky-Books.com

Juvenile non fiction/animals/pets

ISBN - 978-1-62652-432-3
LCCN - Pending - New ISBN

Cover Design & Typeset by Kristeen Wegner
Illustrations by Janice Byer

A portion of every book sold will go toward the building of the Shepherd's Gate Life Center in Livermore, California.

WWW.**HENRY**THE**GREAT**BLUE**HERON**.COM

Printed in the United States of America

Jabberwocky
Books

To my wonderful husband, Lance,

for always being supportive of whatever project I am currently into.

And to George and Sammy for putting up with the sight and smell

of thawing fish in the sink every morning.

I want to make a special mention of the women and children of

Shepherd's Gate who have reminded me how precious a simple smile or hug

really is and that everyone just wants someone to be glad to see them.

They also remind me firsthand how much kids love to be read to . . . even if they

let you get to only page two before running to find another book!

The Most Unusual Pet Ever:

Henry, Our Great Blue Heron

and His Adventures

Well, hi there!

Thank you for wanting to know more about our unusual pet, Henry.

You cannot put him on a leash or take him for a walk.

He does not wear a collar with his name and "if found" information around his neck.

He does not come when you call his name, and you cannot put him in a cage.

You cannot pet him or give him a bath.

He does not sit next to you on the couch or sleep beside you at night.

He will never come into the house and could never be taken to the veterinarian.

But you don't have to follow him picking up his poop either!

THEN HOW IN THE WORLD
CAN WE CALL HIM A PET?

Well we do. And after you read this story, you will realize that a special friend or pet can come in many forms.

So sit back, relax, and enjoy the story!

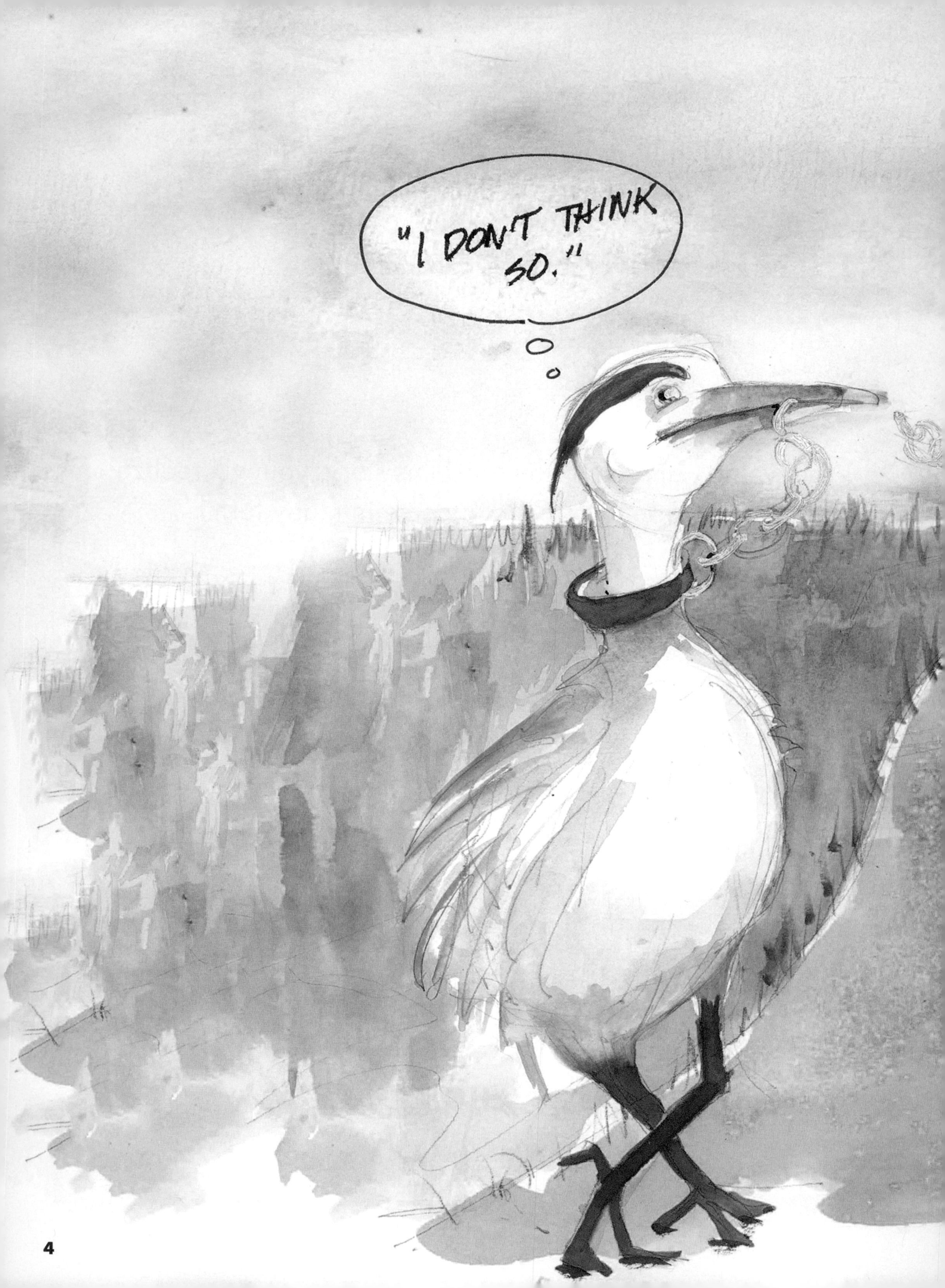
"I DON'T THINK SO."

The Day
We Met
Henry

It was a normal morning at the Perry house. My husband Lance and my two stepchildren George (age 12) and Samantha (age 8) were still in bed. We live in a quiet neighborhood in San Ramon, California, about 25 miles east of San Francisco. Our house is on a corner with a big backyard and two ponds filled with fish *(the fish will become a very important part of the story)*.

I was making coffee when all of a sudden, from the corner of my eye, I notice something big and moving outside. I almost scream! By the small pond is a HUGE bird! I think it's a bird. It looks six feet tall. What is it?

I run to get my camera. (*No one is going to believe this. I need proof!*) I race to the back door with my camera just as the "thing" is flying away. Its wings stretch six feet across. Its long legs dangle behind as it flies away. Oh, what a sight! What was that?

I reach for my "Bird Identification" book to find out. Usually I'm looking up the name of a cute little birdie with red on his head or yellow on his belly. But flipping through the book now I'm thinking this is something big and prehistoric. Will it even be in this book? Then I see what it was: a GREAT BLUE HERON. Wow! How cool is that? Right in our own backyard. Will it ever come back?

The Bird
Is Back!

To my surprise and delight, the Bird was back at the pond within five minutes. The Bird is actually about four feet tall, not six, but hey, that's still big for a bird in our yard. Now the rest of the family is up and can see it for themselves. I didn't need the proof of a photograph after all. We are all excited to see this big Bird in our yard. What's it doing here? Then we realize that it's after the fish in the pond. It grabbed one in its mouth! Oh no! That Bird just swallowed one of our fish!

We shoo the Bird away. He flies off but then comes back. For days we tried to shoo it away for good. We laid screens across the ponds trying to keep the Bird out, but we were afraid its legs would get caught between the screens. No one wants to see a bird get stuck!

Where Did All the Fish Go?

After several days the Bird ate almost all the fish in both ponds. The remaining fish were so afraid they hid and would not even come to the surface to eat their food. I think they felt like they were the food, and they were being tricked to come out so the Bird could eat them. I don't blame them.

Even though this Bird was eating our fish, he wasn't being mean to us. After all, that's what Great Blue Herons do. They eat fish. And we have two big "food bowls" just waiting for him. What a good find for the Bird. And for us too, it turns out.

The First Fish

"Wow, this Bird sure gets an A for effort," I told my husband.

"This Bird must really be hungry. Maybe we should go buy it a fish at the grocery store," my husband said. "That might keep the Bird away from the fish in our ponds."

And that is how it began. We went to the store. We bought a pack of four trout (with their heads on and everything). We laid one on the grass in the backyard, and watched as the Bird quickly grabbed it up with its long beak and swallowed the trout whole.

The Bird flew away after eating the trout, leaving the fish in our ponds alone. Had our plan worked? It seemed so. The Bird kept coming back but only in the morning for a snack of one fish. Then it would fly away again, leaving the ponds alone. After four days I was out of fish. So I went back to the store and bought another pack of four trout. I wasn't sure how long this Bird would continue to come to our yard looking for fish.

Well, that was ten years ago.

The Bird Should Have a Name

We did not know if the Bird was a girl or a boy, but we felt like it was a boy. So we named the Bird "Henry, the Great Blue Heron." Apparently, male herons are about ten percent bigger than the females. Even though we have no other heron to compare Henry to, we feel like he is a boy . . . to us anyway.

Getting to
Know
Each Other

Henry and I both startled each other a lot in the beginning. I was startled when I opened the curtains in the morning to find this BIG BIRD sitting outside the window on top of our barbecue or picnic table. Henry was startled by the sudden opening of the curtains. Frightened and crazy-like, he would open his wings and half fly, half fall to the ground. Who knows how long he had been waiting there.

When Henry regained his composure, he would return to the window and stare at me, waiting. He seemed to be asking, "Where's my fish?"

All this would happen before I had my first cup of coffee. Too early in the morning for such things! But I am always happy to see Henry waiting for me to feed him.

Isn't this what dogs and cats do? Is Henry, this wild bird, starting to act like a pet? A very *unusual* pet.

Our Feeding Routine Begins

In a short time Henry and I got used to each other's presence and settled into our routine. I would open the curtains slowly. Henry, getting into position would walk toward the corner of the grass. I would give a little tap on the glass door and then open it. I'm always talking to Henry as I come out to greet him and give him his fish.

"How are you this morning, Henry?"

Then I would drop the fish on the corner of the grass. As I would turn to go back into the house, Henry would grab it up with his long beak. He then stretches his neck out and down the fish goes, head first. Sometimes Henry flies or runs to the pond with the fish in his mouth and "dips it" into the water before swallowing it. It's quite entertaining!

Over the years Henry has become so comfortable that now he stands right at the sliding glass door and waits patiently. I open the door and drop the fish in front of him. Much easier than walking outside at six in the morning.

Fish, **Fish,** and **More** Fish!

In the last ten years we have gone through a lot of fish. You see, you cannot get trout or smelt at the pet store, so we go to the grocery store. The clerks at our neighborhood grocery store know the crazy story of Henry and are used to our 20-pound fish orders.

While standing in line with a large box of fish or bags of frozen smelt, I am often asked, "How are you going to prepare that?" And again I share the story of Henry the Great Blue Heron with a stranger. The things we do for the ones we love. But it's always worth it!

Sometimes Henry...

Like any other pet, Henry has quirks and a personality all his own. Every day brings something different. Sometimes Henry:

- Stands on the fence while grooming his feathers with his long beak.
- Strolls through my husband's garden walking on the vegetables.
- Hangs out on the roof or chimney for the day, enjoying the view.
- Eats quickly and then flies away.
- Glares at us through the back door for hours, just watching.
- Twists his body and shakes his feathers. He looks four times his size when he does that.
- Curls his long neck into an S shape and rests his head on his body and goes to sleep. He looks only two feet tall when he does that.

- Stands at attention, tilting his head, looking up into the sky. Maybe he sees someone he knows?
- Patiently looks into the pond all day, hoping for a fish perhaps?
- Cools himself off by spreading his wings wide to catch the breeze.
- Gracefully stretches himself out by extending one wing and one leg out at a time.
- Makes a "FRAWK" sound. Is he scared, talking, or wanting more fish?

And then sometimes Henry will not show up in our yard for a few days.

Henry, *Famous?*

On the days when Henry doesn't show up for his snack, we always wonder, "Where is he? Free fish! Silly bird, how can he pass that up?" He must be doing something very important. Maybe he's visiting family or friends? On a vacation?

We started to realize all the times we had seen Henry's likeness on so many different things:

Calendars

Greeting cards

Postcards

Socks and T-shirts

Sculptures and Paintings

Garden decoys

Binocular advertisements

Oceanside hotel logos

Road signs

Jewelry

Bird bingo

There is even a Great Blue Heron beer!

Herons are everywhere! So we had an idea of where Henry might be when he doesn't show up to get his morning snack. He must be at a photo shoot getting his picture taken or his likeness painted. Maybe Henry is a model. Maybe Henry is FAMOUS! Well, he is famous to us.

Does **Henry** Think He Is at the **People Zoo?**

On many days Henry will hang out on the patio, staring at us through the sliding glass door. What is going through his mind? He acts like he's at the zoo.

Think about it:

- He flies in and observes the humans on display through the glass door. Watching and waiting for a human to do something worth looking at. Look, that one is eating. Oh, that one is cleaning the kitchen.
- He places his "snack" order by staring through the glass door, and swallows his snack while still looking at the humans on display. He then gets a beverage, a sip of water at the pond.
- After he tires of the scene, he flies away.

It sounds very much like a trip to the zoo to me.

Henry and the Ducks

Like any other pet, Henry thinks this is HIS yard and does not take kindly to another animal or water bird getting fed through HIS back door. A few years ago, in the Spring, two mallard ducks landed in our backyard. They would stay throughout the day, lounging by the ponds and eating cracked corn (fed to them through the back door). They left in the late afternoon and returned in the morning.

Well, this did not sit well with Henry. He glared at them, sticking his beak out, standing tall, and cornering them to one side of the pond. I was so surprised to see the ducks return the next day, especially after the way Henry had treated them. The two ducks stayed around for a few weeks and then went away.

Who knows if they will be back again next Spring? I hope so. Henry will simply have to work on his manners. There is enough food for everyone, and Henry doesn't even like cracked corn.

And the Chickens!

Yes, chickens! To help with the garden, we brought home three chickens. Their names are Mother, Raven, and Braveheart. They hang out in the garden eating bugs and fertilizing the ground as they go. We think of these "three girls" as Henry's sisters.

Henry is much nicer to his sisters than he was to the visiting ducks. By "nicer" I mean he basically ignores them. Thank goodness because they live here, and it's so much better when everyone can get along. Henry must know that even though these birds have feathers, they are not water birds and will not be competing for his fish. Or maybe he has matured!

I Wish
I Could Talk to Him

Whenever I am around Henry, I talk to him.

"How are you today, Henry?" I ask.

"Where do you go when you fly away from here?"

"Do you have other families to visit? Do they feed you too?"

"Do you sleep in a nest? If you do, where is it?"

"Do you have children?"

"Are you a girl or a boy?"

"How old are you?"

Wouldn't it be great if our pet or any animal could talk to us for five minutes? What would you ask? What would they ask you? Better make it ten minutes.

Just *Glad* to Know *You*

For now I am happy to talk to Henry using actions and behaviors. Unless someone comes up with an animal-to-human communication device, what other choice do I have? I feel Henry is happy when he flies into our yard, eagerly looking for his fish. He seems to be saying to me, "I am healthy, hungry, and glad to know where I can get an easy snack!"

When Henry stands by the pond on one leg, with his head comfortably in an S shape, resting on his body for so many hours, I can see that he is relaxed and must feel safe. That makes me happy.

I hope Henry can hear and feel what I cannot tell him in words. Through my smile and pleasant tone, I hope he knows that I am always happy to see him, and that I care about him and feel blessed by his presence.

He's *Still Wild*

We know and respect the fact that Henry is a wild bird and never want him to stop fending for himself. It would not be good for Henry to rely only on us for his food. Yes, we give him a snack when he comes over, but we are glad to see Henry also hunting for food in the yard. He finds bugs, snails, and grubs. Sometimes I think he might be trying to cover up his fish breath with bugs. Bugs might be breath mints in the bird world!

I wonder what would happen if his heron friends found out about his secret fish spot. Henry has got to keep this to himself! He still looks in the pond for more fish even though there have not been any fish there since he ate them all years ago. But it's fun to watch him. He stares into the water, patiently waiting to see a fish swim by. I guess he has not given up hope, as none of us ever should.

Have You *Ever* Seen a *Great* Blue Heron?

Even with the streams, golf courses with ponds, and the many miles of open space reserved for wildlife around us, I had never noticed a Great Blue Heron in our neighborhood. I'm sure there are more like him. Henry has reminded me to always look up, look down, and look all around! Look in the trees! Look in the bushes!

It is amazing what treasures of nature are around us. All you have to do is stop, look, and listen. Soon you will see and hear what has always been there, so quietly going about its business. Birds and bugs and butterflies too! You never know what you might see.

About the Author

Sondra Perry lives in San Ramon, California, with her husband, Lance. This is Sondra's first children's book. Look for her next two books "Baby Carrots" out in the Fall of 2013, and "Crunchy Carrots" following shortly thereafter. Sondra is available for readings and offers fun and educational presentations to groups of all ages.   sondra.perry4@gmail.com

About the Illustrator

Award-winning artist Janice Byer has a Bachelor of Fine Arts degree from the California College of Arts and Crafts. She is a successful watercolor, pastel, and oil painter.   www.artistjanicebyer.com

Check out www.HenryTheGreatBlueHeron.com
to see more photos and videos of the real Henry.

PHOTO BY SONDRA PERRY

Henry, our *Great Blue Heron*